Piotr Ilyich
TCHAIKOVSKY

VARIATIONS
on a
ROCOCO THEME

FOR

Violoncello & Orchestra

OP. 33

mmo

3773

SUGGESTIONS FOR USING THIS MMO EDITION

WE HAVE TRIED to create a product that will provide you an easy way to learn and perform this piece with a full orchestra in the comfort of your own home. The following MMO features and techniques will help you maximize the effectiveness of the MMO practice and performance system:

Where the soloist begins a movement *solo*, we have provided an introductory measure with subtle taps inserted at the actual tempo before the soloist's entrance. Subtle taps are also included in the accompaniment in passages where tempo changes or is unclear; and these taps are indicated in the printed score.

Chapter stops on your CD are conveniently located throughout the piece at the beginnings of practice sections, and are cross-referenced in the score. This should help you quickly find a desired place in the music as you learn the piece.

Chapter stops have also been placed at orchestra entrances (after cadenzas, for example) so that, with the help of a second person, it is possible to perform a seamless version of the concerto alongside your MMO CD accompaniment. While we have allotted what is generally considered an average amount of time for a cadenza, each performer will have a different interpretation and observe individual tempi. Your personal rendition may preclude a perfect "fit" within the space provided. Therefore, by having a second person press the pause ❙❙ button on your CD player after the start of each cadenza, followed by the next track ▶❙ button, your CD will be cued to the orchestra's re-entry. When you as soloist are at the end of the cadenza or other solo passage, the second person can press the play ▶ (or pause ❙❙ button) on the CD remote to allow a synchronized orchestra re-entry.

Because it involves a fixed orchestral performance, there is an inherent lack of flexibility in tempo and cadenza length. We have observed generally accepted tempi, but some may wish to perform at a different tempo, or to slow down or speed up the accompaniment for practice purposes. In additional to the slow-tempo accompaniments included with this album, you can purchase from MMO specialized CD players and recorders that allows variable speed while maintaining proper pitch. This is an indispensable tool for the serious musician and you may wish to look into purchasing this useful piece of equipment for full enjoyment of all your MMO editions.

We want to provide you with the most useful practice and performance accompaniments possible. If you have any suggestions for improving the MMO system, please feel free to contact us. You can reach us by e-mail at *info@musicminusone.com.*

ABOUT THE 'PRACTICE TEMPO' VERSION

AS AN ALTERNATIVE to the more virtuosic tempi observed in the standard MMO complete and accompaniment versions heard on this album, we have included a second, slow-tempo accompaniment version of the up-tempo variations of the piece. This will allow you to begin at a comfortably reduced speed until fingerings and technique are more firmly in grasp, at which time the full-speed version can be substituted.

Music Minus One

3773

CONTENTS

*Only up-tempo variations are presented in slow-tempo; others are presented at their original speed.

Violoncello Solo

Variations on a Rococo Theme

for Violoncello and Orchestra
op. 33

Edited by
Dominique de Williencourt

Pyotr Ilyich Tchaikovsky
(1840-1893)

Var. II: Tempo del Thema

Var. III: Andante sostenuto

Var. IV: Andante grazioso

800.669.7464 U.S. — 914.592.1188 International

MUSIC MINUS ONE
50 Executive Boulevard
Elmsford, New York 10523-1325
800.669.7464 U.S. — 914.592.1188 International

www.musicminusone.com
info@musicminusone.com